WHAT DO WE BELIEVE?

Workbook

STRIVING for ETERNITY
MINISTRIES

A Ministry of:
Striving for Eternity Ministries
www.StrivingForEternity.org

by Pastor Andrew R. Rappaport

WHAT DO WE BELIEVE?

Lesson 1

Authority

The authority for Christianity is Scripture _____. This is a critical doctrine for Christianity. The only authority for life and godliness is Scripture, not men (i.e. priests or leaders), church, councils or creeds.

The Bible is God's special self-revelation, which is limited in space and time and is directed to various designated individuals (2 Peter 1:21). The accepted books and writings that make up the Bible are the 39 Old Testament and 27 New Testament without any of the additional writings commonly known as the Apocrypha. The Bible provides the only inerrant (without error) and absolutely authoritative propositional knowledge of God that exists.

The authority of Scripture is God's self-revelation of One who has the right and power to command compliance in thought and action upon His rational creatures (Acts 17:30, 31; Romans 15:28). The Scriptures are our ultimate basis of authority for determining what is and who are right and wrong. Therefore, the Bible supremely defines what we are to believe and how we are to conduct ourselves. The Bible alone is authoritative for faith and practice.

I.   Revelation

The term "revelation" refers to the divine act of communicating to man what man otherwise would not know. It is God's self disclosure to man. There are two reasons why revelation was necessary: 1) Because God is, by His nature, inaccessible to man (Isaiah 55:9) and 2) Because of the fall, mankind broke their fellowship with God (Genesis 3:24). In studying the topic of revelation there are two broad categories into which all of our understanding of revelation falls into: _____ revelation and _____ revelation.

Revelation is progressive with its final manifestation in the person of Jesus Christ. The revelation of God did not come to one person at one time. It was a progression of revelation to many people over 1,500 years.

A.   Natural Revelation

Natural Revelation uses natural phenomena as means of revealing God. The two instruments through which God reveal Himself to all of mankind are nature and conscience. Nature clearly reveals God in a universal and timeless manner (Psalm 8:1-3; 19:1-6; Isaiah 40:12-14; Acts 14:12-17; Romans 1:19-21). The conscience convinces individuals of moral right and wrong thoughts and behaviors (Romans 2:14-15; 9:1-2; 13:5; 1 Peter 2:19; 1 Corinthians 8:7, 10, 12; 2 Corinthians 1:12; 4:2).

The purpose of natural revelation is to render man _____
to the existence of God and prepare the way for special revelation.
Natural revelation is limited in its ability to inform the individuals about
redemption (Romans 10:13-17).

B.   *Special Revelation*

Revelation which is the intervention into the natural course of things, and
which is supernatural both as to the _____ and the _____.
Special revelation is supernatural, propositional and redemptive. Special
revelation is uniquely of God and often misunderstood or twisted by many
religions or cults.

The Bible is the form of special revelation that God uses today to
communicate to people. However, in the Bible we see Theophonies and
Anthropomorphisms.

1.   *Theophonies*

A theophony is a physical manifestation of God in some way. It
could be manifested in nature (Exodus 13:21-22), auditory (Exodus
19:1-3) or bodily (Genesis 16:7-14; 31:11-18; Joshua 5:13-15).
Many religious leaders claim to has theophonies. However, there
are two important facts about a true theophony.

a.   **The _____ of the person**

The Bible records examples of people experiencing
theophonies. The response of the person is one of awe and
worship (Isaiah 6:5; Revelation 1:17). Anyone who sees or
hears a theophony responses is a manor fitting of being in
the presence of the Most Holy, Supremely Divine God of the
Universe.

b.   **The _____ of the person**

The message of the person who sees or hears a true
theophony is ALWAYS consistent with Scripture and NEVER
contradicts it (2 Corinthians 13:8). The message must be
compared with the Scriptures for accuracy (Acts 17:11; 1
John 4:1-3). The person who receives a true theophony
would not be concerned if someone wants to compare the
message with Scripture. However, if a leader expects trust
explicitly without questioning, then the message is not from
God, because the leader is purporting themselves to be the
authority and not the Scriptures.

2.   *Anthropomorphisms*

Anthropomorphism is a **figure of speech**, not to be understood
literally, used by writers of Scripture in which _____
physical characters are attributed to God for the sake of illustrating

an important point. For example, Scripture sometimes speaks of the "face" or "arm" of God, even though God is revealed to be Spirit and not limited in time and space by the constraints of a physical body. Anthropomorphisms essentially help to make an otherwise abstract truth about God more concrete. However, God is not a physical being, He is Spirit (John 4:24). It is an error to understand anthropomorphisms as literally assuming God to have a physical body. God the Father is not a man, nor was He one.

To believe that based upon the anthropomorphisms God is a man ignores the descriptions of God as an animal. God is also described as having _____ like a bird (Psalms 36:7; 57:1; 61:4; 63:7; 91:4). If someone teaches that God has a physical body, based on anthropomorphisms, then to be consistent, God would also have to be considered a bird or some half man – half bird.

II.   Inspiration

_____ Scripture is inspired by God. Inspiration is from a Greek compound word which mean _____. All Scripture is breathed or spoken from the mouth of God to mankind. It is the writings and not the writers that were inspired.

Definition:

Inspiration identifies that supernatural work of the Holy Spirit in which He superintended (controlled and directed) the reception (to the writers) and communication (to the hearers and the writing) of the divine message to mankind such that the product (the original writing) is verbally (every word) and plenary (completely) both inerrant (without error) and authoritative.

"All Scripture is given by inspiration of God, and is profitable for doctrine, for reproof, for correction, for instruction in righteousness" (2 Timothy 3:16).

God spoke in His written Word by a process of dual authorship. The Holy Spirit so superintended the human authors that, through their individual personalities and different styles of writing, they composed and recorded God's Word to man (2 Peter 1:20-21) without error in the whole or in the part (Matthew 5:18; 2 Timothy 3:16). Thus, the Scriptures are completely and totally sufficient for life and godliness.

"knowing this first, that no prophecy of Scripture is of any private interpretation, for prophecy never came by the will of man, but holy men of God spoke as they were moved by the Holy Spirit" (2 Peter 1:20-21)

By virtue that the Scriptures are inspired by God they were part of the canon. Men only _____ the canonical books; they did not inspire them nor declare them inspired. They were inspired whether mankind recognized it or not.

III. Sufficiency

The Word of God is completely and totally _____ for the believer in every area of life. The Scriptures are all that is necessary for the completing and maturing of the man of God.

> *"All Scripture is given by inspiration of God, and is profitable for doctrine, for reproof, for correction, for instruction in righteousness, that the man of God may be complete, thoroughly equipped for every good work"* (2 Timothy 3:16-17).

There is absolutely no human _____ that needs to be added to or replace the Scriptures to meet the needs of the believer for life and living. God commands that no part, no matter how small, should ever be added nor subtracted from the Bible (Deuteronomy 4:2; 12:32; Proverbs 30:6; Jeremiah 26:2; Revelation 22:18-19). It is totally complete and sufficient for every area of life for every generation. The Scriptures are sufficient for life and godliness. The Bible constitutes the only infallible rule of faith and practice (Matthew 5:18; 24:35; John 10:35; 16:12-13; 17:17; 1 Corinthians 2:13; 2 Timothy 3:15-17; Hebrews 4:12; 2 Peter 1:20-21).

According to 2 Peter 1:16-19, the Scriptures are a more certain determiner of truth than hearing the voice of God and definitely more then the voice of any person.

> *16 For we were not making up clever stories when we told you about the power of our Lord Jesus Christ and his coming again. We have seen his majestic splendor with our own eyes. 17 And he received honor and glory from God the Father when God's glorious, majestic voice called down from heaven, "This is my beloved Son; I am fully pleased with him." 18 We ourselves heard the voice when we were there with him on the holy mountain. 19 Because of that, we have even greater confidence in the message proclaimed by the prophets. Pay close attention to what they wrote, for their words are like a light shining in a dark place—until the day Christ appears and his brilliant light shines in your hearts.*

Therefore, it is the Scriptures alone that are our ultimate basis of authority for determining what and what is right and wrong.

IV. Interpretation

The Scriptures where written to be _____. One of the ministries of the Holy Spirit is to illuminate the Scriptures to the mind of the child of God. The Holy Spirit indwells every believer. Therefore, true Christians do not need a "priest" to interpret for them. They are priests and all have the same Holy Spirit indwelling them. It is the role of the Christian to diligently study to show themselves approved unto God (2 Timothy 2:15; Acts 17:11) and the Holy Spirit will reveal the meaning of the Scriptures (1 Corinthians 2:4).

Since, the Bible is a progressive revelation, it is important to interpret the Bible as a progression of revelation to come to a proper interpretation. Not all the Bible applies to us today. We must interpret it in an understanding of what it meant when it was written to know if it contains principals for life today.

Any cult will teach that the individual member _____ interpret the Scriptures without the leader or chief members of the organization. It is this authoritarian view that is one of the defining traits of a cult.

Thought Questions

1. Why does the role of the Holy Spirit illuminating the Christian make Scripture the ultimate authority for the Christian?

2. Does position in the church grant an individual more of an understanding of the Scriptures then any other believing member of the church?

3. Does "the church" have authority over the individual believer? Why or why not?

4. What is the source of Christian authority in this world? Why?

5. A friend tells you that you need a priest to interpret the Scriptures. How do you correct this belief?

Lesson 2

Biblical Reliability

Biblical reliability is an important topic to understand because many attack Christianity due to a lack of understanding about how the Bible came to be. Many try to claim that we cannot trust the Bible, but it is our only authority from God. The only way that we can know about God objectively and absolutely is if He reveals Himself to us in some form of universal communication. The presupposition of Christianity is that God exists, and He has spoken.

I. Refuting the Critics

A. The Issue of Trust

Non-believers challenge that the Bible cannot be _____ because men wrote it. However, men have written everything we know, and they trust those things that they have learned from men. We believe and trust in an _____ Author, which is why Christians get their authority from the Word of God alone, Sola scriptura.

B. Variants

The Bible is without error and without flaw in the original writings, but the challenge is that we do not have any original manuscripts of the Bible. Additionally, the many manuscripts that we have today have some _____ between them.

Daniel Wallace states, "A textual variant is simply any difference from a standard text (e.g., a printed text, a particular manuscript, etc.) that involves spelling, word order, omission, addition, substitution, or a total rewrite of the text." Each time that we have a variant between manuscripts, it becomes what is called a "variant reading."

Scholars argue that the number of variant readings is about _____ in the New Testament. That sounds like a large number, especially when you consider that there are only about 138,200 words in the Greek New Testament. The reason for this is that scholars count each change, even of the same word between multiple manuscripts, as an individual variant.

Due to the large number of manuscripts, we can identify where these changes occurred, and this knowledge reveals that not a single Biblical doctrine is affected by these variants. Furthermore, with most of these changes, we can more easily determine the original meaning of the text.

II.   Category of Variants

A.   *Spelling or Punctuation*

It is helpful to define the types of variants. The majority of these variants , 75%, are "_____ errors or punctuation." While the misspelling of words can change the meaning of a text base the context can often determine the correct meaning. So, in most cases of these spelling errors, we can easily conclude which is the original.

B.   *Not Meaningful but Viable*

The second largest category of variant, 19%, is "not _____ but viable." Viable means that we cannot get back to the original text. This means that the variant does not change the meaning of the text in any way.

C.   *Meaningful but Not Viable*

The third largest category, 5%, is those variants that are "meaningful but not _____." Therefore, with these variants, the only way we can get back to the original text is either by the context or, more often, from the numbers of other manuscripts to which we can compare the variant.

D.   *Meaningful and Viable*

The last type of variant is the _____—less than 1%—but the most significant: "meaningful and viable." These are the only ones that present a problem for Biblical scholars and those who do textual criticism because 1) they do affect the meaning of the text and 2) we cannot get back to the original text.

In summary, out of all of the variants, 99% of them either do not impact the meaning of the text or can be traced back to the original meaning. Consequently, only 1% of the variants need to concern us.

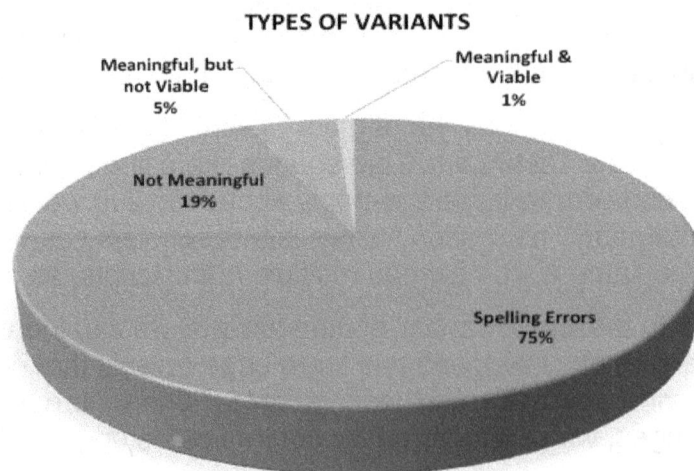

TYPES OF VARIANTS

Meaningful, but not Viable 5%

Meaningful & Viable 1%

Not Meaningful 19%

Spelling Errors 75%

III.   Dispelling the Myth

The Bible translation was not like the "_____ game," where one person makes one copy with a few mistakes and passes it along to another person who would make another copy but with some more mistakes and so on until the final product is nothing like the original. They did not play the "telephone game," where you have only one person handling the message at a time and passing on a corrupted version of what they received.

The copyists would make multiple copies and give it to others to make multiple copies. These copies were spread throughout the region so that they could be duplicated and circulated farther. Subsequently, when there were changes from copy to copy, each copy could be traced to its geographical location so that it could be seen how this change was fostered. The main difference between this process and the "telephone game" is that these copies are written down and not auditory. For that reason, each one can be checked and verified against original or older manuscripts.

IV.   Factors for Reliability

A.   *Closeness of the Copy to the Original Writing*

Changes occur over time: the less time that you have, the _____ changes you should have. The closer a copy is to the original, the less likely it is that it contains changes. Using the age of the manuscript allows us to assume that there would be fewer changes.

B.   *Number of Manuscripts*

Examining all of the manuscripts, the best guess is that we have over _____ manuscripts of the New Testament. However, if we did not use any of these manuscripts, we could recreate the whole of the New Testament, except for 11 verses, from the quotations of the early church fathers alone during AD 150-200. There are over 1 million quotations from the early church fathers. When we add all the manuscripts, fragments, and quotations from the New Testament, it approaches almost 70,000 copies. Suddenly, we have a very large number of New Testament references. It should be clear at this point that the common argument that the Bible was later edited and disseminated around the world in AD 300-500 is false.

C.   *Geographical Location*

The geographical location helps to see if a variant occurs only in one area compared to the rest of the world, we assume that one area is the error.

With all this information, we can rest on the fact that very little of the New Testament is in question, and even less of the Old Testament is. Due to the very large number of manuscripts, it helps us identify every possible variant location in the Bible, and, because of that, we know that not one of them affects any major Christian doctrine.

Thought Questions

1. How can you respond to someone that claims that the Bible cannot be trusted because it was developed like the "telephone game"?

2. How does the age of a manuscript affect its trustworthiness?

3. How does the number of manuscripts affect its trustworthiness?

4. How does the geographical loaction of manuscripts affect its trustworthiness?

5. How trustworthy is the Bible?

Lesson 3

God

There is _____ living and true God (Deuteronomy 6:4; Isaiah 45:5-7; 1 Corinthians 8:4), an infinite, all knowing Spirit (John 4:24), perfect in all His attributes, one in essence, eternally existing in three Persons: Father, Son, and Holy Spirit (Matthew 28:19; 2 Corinthians 13:14), each equally deserving worship and obedience.

V. Description

A. *God's Attributes*

God orders and disposes all things according to His own purpose and grace (Psalm 145:8-9; 1 Corinthians 8:6). He is the Creator of all things (Genesis 1:1-31; Ephesians 3:9). As the only absolute and omnipotent Ruler in the universe, He is sovereign in creation, providence, and redemption (Psalm 103:19; Romans 11:36).

He has an all-inclusive plan that He designed for His own _____ all things that come to pass (Ephesians 1:11). He continually upholds, directs and governs all creatures and events (1 Chronicles 29:11).

In His sovereignty He is neither author nor approver of sin (Habakkuk 1:13; John 8:38-47), nor does He abridge the accountability of moral, intelligent creatures (1 Peter 1:17). He has graciously chosen from eternity past those whom He would have as His own (Ephesians 1:4-6); He saves from sin all who come to Him through Jesus Christ; He adopts as his own all those who come to Him (John 1:12; Romans 8:15; Galatians 4:5; Hebrews 12:5-9).

B. *God is Not a Man*

The essence of God is totally and completely _____. This is the invisible source of personality (John 1:18; Romans 1:20; Colossians 1:15; 1 Timothy 1:17; 6:15-16). God is not physical or material. Thus, God is not dependent, limited, restricted or subject to matter or space in anyway. God's Spirit is immense and omnipresent. As applied to God, God is infinite in matter.

Statements in Scripture that refer to God in physical forms are called "anthropomorphic expressions". They are figures of speech, which assist men to better understand God and/or His acts; they do not ascribe bodily parts. When Scripture states that God appears to men in time past as a physical being, these statements are called "Theophonies". Theophonies were divine _____, adjustments for man, not glimpses of God.

VI. Triunity

The terms T*rinity, Triunity* or *Trinitarian* are not found in Scripture, but are terms we use to describe the teaching that God is one in essence yet existing in three personalities. The Triunity refers to the doctrine of the three _____ in one _____. Some falsely, define this doctrine as three Persons in one Person or three Gods in one God. Both are incorrect. These false definitions are used by false teachers to make it easy to improperly refute this doctrine (i.e. a straw man argument). Properly defined, **the Triunity is three individuals, separate and distinct Persons in one completely and totally unified Godhead** (1 John 5:7).

The concept of the Triunity is incomprehensible to man. All the attributes of God are fully true of each of the Persons or Essences of the Godhead. The doctrine of the Triunity is further proven in the doctrines of the Deity of Christ and the Deity of the Holy Spirit.

A. *HINTS OF THE TRINITY IN THE OLD TESTAMENT*

The Old Testament emphasis is clearly the uniqueness and unity of God. This foundation in understanding God was necessary in order to refute the primary religious deviation at the time, _____. However, even though the Old Testament emphasizes the unity of God, we still find hints to the truth of the Triunity.

1. *The Use of* _____

   In the beginning God [Elohim] created the heavens and the earth. (Genesis 1:1).

   Elohim, a plural noun, is used with singular verbs as it is employed to describe the one true God. We thus see that this name teaches the unity of God and allows for the teaching of the Triunity of God.

2. *The Use of* _____ _____

   God also used plural pronouns to refer to Himself (Genesis 1:26; 3:22; Isaiah 6:8). These intimations support the plurality of the Godhead.

   Genesis 1:26

   > *Then God said, "Let Us make man in Our image, according to Our likeness; let them have dominion over the fish of the sea, over the birds of the air, and over the cattle, over all the earth and over every creeping thing that creeps on the earth."*

Genesis 3:22

> *Then the Lord God said, "Behold, the man has become like one of Us, to know good and evil. And now, lest he put out his hand and take also of the tree of life, and eat, and live forever"—*

Isaiah 6:8

> *Also I heard the voice of the Lord, saying: "Whom shall I send, And who will go for Us? Then I said, Here am I! Send me."*

3. *The Use of _____*

Many who oppose the doctrine of the Triunity claim that it contradicts the clear teaching of the Bible that there is but one God. The word used in Deuteronomy 6:4, *"Hear, O Israel: The Lord our God, the Lord is one"*, which is translated as "one" (echad), does not refer to oneness in the sense of _____, but oneness in the sense _____.

The Hebrew word echad is used as one as a single only in counting or when there is a subject after the word. In the cases when it is used to refer to God the subject, being God, is before the word, echad. In those cases the word is there to emphasize unity and not singleness.

B. *TEACHING ABOUT THE TRINITY IN THE NEW TESTAMENT*

While the Old Testament emphasized the _____ of God and at the time allowed for the teaching of the Triunity, the New Testament clearly presents the Godhead as one in essence, yet existing in three persons.

1. *Three Persons are Recognized as _____*

   a. **The Father is Recognized as God**

   John 16:27

   > *for the Father Himself loves you, because you have loved Me, and have believed that I came forth from God.*

b. The Son is Recognized as God

John 1:1

In the beginning was the Word, and the Word was with God, and the Word was God.

John 8:58

Jesus said to them, "Most assuredly, I say to you, before Abraham was, I AM."

John 20:26-29

[26] And after eight days His disciples were again inside, and Thomas with them. Jesus came, the doors being shut, and stood in the midst, and said, "Peace to you!" [27] Then He said to Thomas, "Reach your finger here, and look at My hands; and reach your hand here, and put it into My side. Do not be unbelieving, but believing." [28] And Thomas answered and said to Him, "My Lord and my God!" [29] Jesus said to him, "Thomas, because you have seen Me, you have believed. Blessed are those who have not seen and yet have believed."

c. The Spirit is Recognized as God

Acts 5:3-4

[3] But Peter said, "'Ananias, why has Satan filled your heart to lie to the Holy Spirit and keep back part of the price of the land for yourself? [4] While it remained, was it not your own? And after it was sold, was it not in your own control? Why have you conceived this thing in your heart? You have not lied to men but to God.'"

2. The Three Personalities are seen in _____ with each other

Matthew 28:19

Go therefore and make disciples of all the nations, baptizing them in the name of the Father and of the Son and of the Holy Spirit,

2 Corinthians 13:4

For though He was crucified in weakness, yet He lives by the power of God. For we also are weak in Him, but we shall live with Him by the power of God toward you.

Titus 3:4-7

⁴ But when the kindness and the love of God our Savior toward man appeared, ⁵ not by works of righteousness which we have done, but according to His mercy He saved us, through the washing of regeneration and renewing of the Holy Spirit, ⁶ whom He poured out on us abundantly through Jesus Christ our Savior, ⁷ that having been justified by His grace we should become heirs according to the hope of eternal life.

1 Peter 1:2

elect according to the foreknowledge of God the Father, in sanctification of the Spirit, for obedience and sprinkling of the blood of Jesus Christ: Grace to you and peace be multiplied.

3.   *Three are One in _____*

Each of the Persons of the Triunity are objects of worship (Exodus 20:3; Matthew 14:33; John 4:24; 10:33; Luke 24:51-52; Philippians 2:9-11). They each possess all the attributes of God.

a.   **The Father is One with the Son**

John 1:1

In the beginning was the Word, and the Word was with God, and the Word was God.

John 10:30

I and My Father are one.

John 14:3-9

³ And if I go and prepare a place for you, I will come again and receive you to Myself; that where I am, there you may be also. ⁴ And where I go you know, and the way you know." ⁵ Thomas said to Him, "Lord, we do not know where You are going, and how can we know the way?" ⁶

Jesus said to him, "I am the way, the truth, and the life. No one comes to the Father except through Me. [7] "If you had known Me, you would have known My Father also; and from now on you know Him and have seen Him." [8] Philip said to Him, "Lord, show us the Father, and it is sufficient for us." [9] Jesus said to him, "Have I been with you so long, and yet you have not known Me, Philip? He who has seen Me has seen the Father; so how can you say, 'Show us the Father'?

John 14:23

Jesus answered and said to him, "If anyone loves Me, he will keep My word; and My Father will love him, and We will come to him and make Our home with him.

b.   The Spirit is One with the Son

Romans 8:8-11

[8] So then, those who are in the flesh cannot please God. [9] But you are not in the flesh but in the Spirit, if indeed the Spirit of God dwells in you. Now if anyone does not have the Spirit of Christ, he is not His. [10] And if Christ is in you, the body is dead because of sin, but the Spirit is life because of righteousness. [11] But if the Spirit of Him who raised Jesus from the dead dwells in you, He who raised Christ from the dead will also give life to your mortal bodies through His Spirit who dwells in you.

John 16:13-15

[13] However, when He, the Spirit of truth, has come, He will guide you into all truth; for He will not speak on His own authority, but whatever He hears He will speak; and He will tell you things to come. [14] He will glorify Me, for He will take of what is Mine and declare it to you. [15] All things that the Father has are Mine. Therefore I said that He will take of Mine and declare it to you.

c.   The Spirit is One with the Father

Acts 5:3-4

[3] But Peter said, "Ananias, why has Satan filled your heart to lie to the Holy Spirit and keep back part of the price of

the land for yourself? ⁴ While it remained, was it not your own? And after it was sold, was it not in your own control? Why have you conceived this thing in your heart? You have not lied to men but to God."

Romans 8:8-11

> *⁸ So then, those who are in the flesh cannot please God. ⁹ But you are not in the flesh but in the Spirit, if indeed the Spirit of God dwells in you. Now if anyone does not have the Spirit of Christ, he is not His. ¹⁰ And if Christ is in you, the body is dead because of sin, but the Spirit is life because of righteousness. ¹¹ But if the Spirit of Him who raised Jesus from the dead dwells in you, He who raised Christ from the dead will also give life to your mortal bodies through His Spirit who dwells in you.*

4.   *Three are _____ from Each Other*
There is a unity in the Triunity yet the plurality of the Godhead is distinct from each other (Genesis 1:1-2; 19:24; Psalm 45:6-7; 110:1; Isaiah 63:7,10; Hosea 1:7; John 14:16-17, 28; Galatians 4:4). Distinction in _____ does not mean there is distinction in essence.

a.   **Father is distinct from the Son**

John 14:28 (c.f. Philippians 2:5-8)

> *You have heard Me say to you, 'I am going away and coming back to you.' If you loved Me, you would rejoice because I said, 'I am going to the Father,' for My Father is greater than I.*

Philippians 2:5-8

> *⁵ Let this mind be in you which was also in Christ Jesus, ⁶ who, being in the form of God, did not consider it robbery to be equal with God, ⁷ but made Himself of no reputation, taking the form of a bondservant, and coming in the likeness of men. ⁸ And being found in appearance as a man, He humbled Himself and became obedient to the point of death, even the death of the cross.*

Galatians 4:4

But when the fullness of the time had come, God sent forth His Son, born of a woman, born under the law

b.   Spirit is distinct from Father and Son

John 14:16-17

[16] And I will pray the Father, and He will give you another Helper, that He may abide with you forever— [17] the Spirit of truth, whom the world cannot receive, because it neither sees Him nor knows Him; but you know Him, for He dwells with you and will be in you.

These three persons of the Godhead who are all considered divine are to be recognized as _____ in _____, equally existing in three _____.

NOTE: Many who deny the Trinity do so because they cannot explain it from a human perspective. Yet there are many things about God that are completely beyond our comprehension (i.e., hears and answers all prayer; everywhere at the same time; knows all things; past, present, future and possible in one present reality). No human can explain these things. We believe them because the Bible teaches these truths. The Bible teaches the reality of the Triunity of God, therefore we believe it whether we can explain it or not!

Thought Questions

1. What is the proper definition of the Triunity of God? Support this with Scripture.

2. Why does the Old Testament not explicitly describe the Triunity?

3. Why is it important to study and understand the attributes of God and the Triunity?

4. How can you use this lesson to explain the Triunity to a Jehovah Witness?

5. Why does the Bible sometimes describe God as if He was a man? How do we know that He is not?

Lesson 4

Jesus Christ

Although it has been difficult for men to understand throughout the ages, the Scriptures teach that Jesus Christ is fully _____ and fully _____; two natures in indivisible oneness. It is usually one of the two natures of Christ that are attacked or misunderstood. It is important to realize that Jesus Christ has two natures, one fully man and one fully God. Part of the reason for the confusion is that Jesus at times speaks from the _____ of His humanity even though He is God (Matthew 4:2; Luke 22:43; John 4:6; 19:28).

In the first century Christ's Deity was not questioned but His humanity was. Now it is mostly His Deity that is questioned and not His humanity. It is important to see that the Scriptures clearly teach that Jesus Christ is both God and man; the God-man.

I. The Deity of Christ

In the first centuries after Christ, people did not question the Deity of Jesus Christ. However, after the "Christianization" of the Roman Empire a struggle ensued on the issue. Since that time cults have arisen that have questioned the Deity of Jesus Christ. The Scriptures explicitly prove of the Deity of Jesus Christ by the names, works and attributes of Christ.

A. THE NAMES OF CHRIST INDICATE HIS DEITY

When the Scriptures refer to someone by name it indicates much more about the person then how to refer to them or a title. It indicates their position, personality and character. When comparing the Old and the New Testaments, many names refer to Jesus Christ. These names display His Deity.

1. The Names of Christ in the Old Testament

In the Old Testament we see that future Messiah or Christ is called

1) *"Mighty God"* and *"Everlasting Father"* (Isaiah 9:6),

2) *"Lord"* (Psalm 110:1),

3) *"Immanuel"*, which means "God with us" (Isaiah 7:14) and

4) *"YHWH"* or *"Jehovah"* (Jeremiah 23:6; Isaiah 40:3), a name that is only used of God.

These names all point to the fact that the future Jewish Messiah was to be God Himself.

The reference to Jehovah in Jeremiah 23:5 states, *"'Behold the days are coming', says the Lord, 'that I will raise to David a Branch of righteousness; a King shall reign and prosper, and execute judgment and righteousness in the earth."* The reference of a Branch of David and a King who will prosper and execute judgment is a prophecy of the Messiah's reign. He will reign with righteousness and that is why in verse 6 it says, *"now this is His name by which He will be called: THE _____ OUR RIGHTEOUSNESS"*. It is not a proper name but a description of who He is and how He will reign.

2.   *His Names in the New Testament*

In the New Testament, the names of Jesus Christ are explicitly of Christ. The New Testament calls Jesus *"the Christ"* (Matthew 16:16, 20; 23:8; 24:5; Luke 9:20; John 7:26-42; 11:27). This is the Greek word for "anointed", which in Hebrew is the word "Messiah". The definite article before Christ means that He is the One awaited Messiah prophesied about in the Old Testament.

Scripture refers to Jesus Christ as:

      1) *"God"* (John 1:1, 20:24-29; 1 Timothy 1:1; 4:10; Titus 1:3-4; 2:10, 13; 3:4, 6),

      2) *"Lord"* (Luke 6:46; 24:34; Mark 2:23-28; John 13:13; Acts 10:36; 26:15; Revelation 19:16),

      3) *"Son of God"* (Matthew 16:16; Mark 1:11; 5:7; 15:39; John 10:31-39),

      4) *"First and Last"* (Revelation 1:11, 17; 2:8; 22:13),

      5) *"the Word"* (John 1:1, 14; Revelation 19:13),

      6) *"I AM"* (John 8:58-59) and

      7) *"Savior"* (Titus 1:3-4; 3:4-6).

The phase *"Son of God"* is often misunderstood, because people do not take the time to understand "sonship" in the times and culture of Christ. The word *"son"*, while it can mean _____, most often is used to refer to one who partakes of or is _____ with the one to whom he is son. Some examples of this usage are:

      Sons of Thunder (Mark 3:17)
      Son of Perdition (John 17:12; 2 Thessalonians 2:3)
      Son of Encouragement (Acts 4:36)

Also, note that *"sonship"* in relation to Christ is always connected to his incarnation.

When Jesus Christ uses the name "I AM" it is an explicit reference to Deity (John 8:58-59). In the Greek the phase for "I AM" is the same as the Hebrew for the name of God in Exodus 3:14 often translated YHWH or Jehovah. The Jews at the time of Christ understood this because after using this name about Himself in John 8:58 the Jews *"took up stones to throw at Him"* (v. 59) for blasphemy (calling Himself God) (John 10:33).

B. *THE WORKS OF CHRIST INDICATE HIS DEITY*

The works Jesus Christ did while on earth indicate His Deity. It was one of the proofs or witnesses that He refers other to examine (John 9:3-5). He did things only God could do, such as:

1) Creation (John 1:3; 1 Corinthians 8:6; Ephesians 3:9; Colossians 1:16; Hebrews 1:2)

2) Forgiveness of Sins (Matthew 9:2-6; Mark 2:7)

3) Giving of Life

A) Physical Life (John 11:17, 34-44)

B) Eternal Life (John 10:58)

4) Acceptance of Worship (Matthew 14:33; Luke 24:51-52; Philippians 2:9-11)

5) Judgment of Mankind (John 5:22, 27; Acts 10:42; 2 Timothy 4:1)

C. *THE ATTRIBUTES OF CHRIST INDICATE HIS DEITY*

If Jesus Christ is Deity then He should have the attributes of Deity. There are attributes that are only attributed to God. Therefore, if Christ possesses these attributes it is only because He is _____. In the New Testament we see that Jesus Christ possesses the following attributes of Deity:

1) Incomprehensibility (Ephesian 3:8, 19)

2) Sovereignty (Romans 14:10-12)

3) Omniscience (John 2:24-25; 16:30-32)

4) Omnipotence (John 5:19, 21; Colossians 1:17)

5) Omnipresence (Matthew 29:20; Hebrews 4:13)

6) Immutability (Hebrews 13:8)

7) Eternality (John 1:1; 8:58; Revelation 1:8)

8) Holiness (Mark 1:24)

While possessing the attributes of Deity, Jesus Christ did not necessarily use the attributes of His Deity, but limited Himself by his humanness (Matthew 4:2; Luke 22:43; John 4:6; 19:28). This does not mean that He stopped being God nor was never God, but that somehow He limited Himself to being a man.

> *⁵ Let this mind be in you which was also in Christ Jesus, ⁶ who, being in the form of God, did not consider it robbery to be equal with God, ⁷ but made Himself of no reputation, taking the form of a bondservant, and coming in the likeness of men. ⁸ And being found in appearance as a man, He humbled Himself and became obedient to the point of death, even the death of the cross.* (Philippians 2:5-8)

One passage which ascribes to Christ one of the greatest statements of Deity is Colossians 2:9, *"For in Him dwells all the fullness of the Godhead bodily"*.

After examining the totality of information on the deity of Christ, one must say He is one of three things:

1. _____ – That is, He deceived those who followed Him, telling them He was God.

2. _____ – That is, he was so deluded He did not know what He was saying, claiming to be God.

3. _____ – He was who He said He was "The King of Kings and the Lord of Lords"

II.   The Humanity of Christ

While the Deity of Jesus Christ is widely debated, His humanity seems to be widely accepted as fact. However, there are areas of the humanity of Christ that are still misunderstood by different world religions and cults. It is important to look at the purpose, prior existence, evidence and exaltation of the humanity of Christ.

A.   *The Purpose of the Humanity of Christ*

Why did Jesus Christ have to enter into humanity? Being God, Jesus Christ had everything in Heaven where the angels worshiped Him and there is no sin. However, Jesus Christ came to earth to become a man and live among His creation for the purpose of the His death, burial and resurrection. However, there is more to His purpose then just the cross to the accession.

Christ's death, burial and resurrection provided a _____ for sin (2 Corinthians 5:21). Christ's sacrifice was the payment for our sin so that we could be set free (Romans 6:18, 22). Jesus Christ becomes the fullest revelation of God to man, because *"no one has seen God at any time"* (John 1:18). Now Jesus Christ acts as the only true _____ between God and man (1 Timothy 2:5; 1 John 2:1-2).

The true mediation of Jesus Christ is because He is the only God-man. It is this reality that make Him a _____ High Priest

(Hebrews 2:17-18; 4:14-16). Jesus Christ was the perfect man. He is the ONLY human to have NEVER sinned. His sinlessness is what makes Him a perfect _____ to follow (Philippians 2:5; 1 Peter 2:21), yet as a sympathetic High Priest. It is because He is fully human that He can sympathize with humanity. As a sinless being, He provides a perfect sacrifice for sin. Thus, we can only obtain salvation from God accepting Jesus as a sacrifice if His was sinless. Otherwise, He would have to pay for His own sins, which would disqualify Him as our substitute.

B.   *The Prior Existence of the Humanity of Christ*

Some falsely teach that Jesus Christ was merely a _____ _____. We have seen in the Deity of Christ that He could not be a just a man, good or otherwise. There are others that teach that Jesus Christ during His time on earth or prior was an _____. His Deity disproves this theory as well. If Jesus Christ was at any point in time an angel, He could never have been the Creator of all things.

The correct view of Jesus Christ prior to His humanity, is that He was and is God (John 8:56-59).

> *56 Your father Abraham rejoiced to see My day, and he saw it and was glad." 57 Then the Jews said to Him, "You are not yet fifty years old, and have You seen Abraham?" 58 Jesus said to them, "Most assuredly, I say to you, before Abraham was, I AM." 59 Then they took up stones to throw at Him; but Jesus hid Himself and went out of the temple, going through the midst of them, and so passed by.*

Jesus Christ always was, is and will be God. Those that see Christ as merely a "good man", (Jewish position) believe that Christ came into being at His birth. Those that see Christ as being an angel, (Jehovah Witness position) believe that Christ was in the form of another being before His birth. Jesus Christ claimed that during Abraham's lifetime He was the great "I AM".

C.   *The Evidence of the Humanity of Christ*

There are three evidences of the humanity of Christ.

He possesses the _____ of humanity.

He possesses the _____ of humanity.

He possesses the _____ of humanity.

Jesus Christ has the necessities of humanity a physical body (Hebrews 2:14) and an immaterial soul (Matthew 28:6; Luke 23:46). The reason this is important to note is that the first century Christians were battling the false belief that Jesus Christ did not have a physical body. So when we see much attention giving to Christ's humanity in the later writings, like 1

John, it is because John is trying to combat this false doctrine, not trying to disprove the Deity of Christ. That was widely accepted at the time.

Jesus also possesses the name of humanity. He most often called Himself the *"Son of Man"*, emphasizing His humanity (Matthew 8:20; 9:6; 12:8; Mark 8:31, 38; Luke 19:10; John 6:27, 53, 62). He was also referred to as a *"man"* (John 8:40; 1 Timothy 2:5).

Lastly, He possesses the nature of humanity. Jesus Christ had emotions. We see Him displaying anger (Mark 3:5), compassion (John 13:23) and sorrow (John 11:35). Jesus has the limitations that are common with a human nature, such as, hunger (Matthew 4:2), thirst (John 19:28), fatigue (John 4:6), exhaustion (Luke 22:43), being bound by time (Mark 11:13) and even experiencing death (John 19:30).

D.   *The Exaltation of the Humanity of Christ*

The exaltation of the humanity of Jesus Christ deals with the crucifixion and resurrection of Christ. The purpose of the crucifixion of Jesus Christ was accomplished voluntarily and obediently by the second Person of the Godhead for the substitutionary atonement of the sins of the human race. Historically it is known that Jesus Christ would have died on a cross not a stake, and that it was Jesus Christ on that cross.

The resurrection is evidenced by the scriptural testimony (1 Corinthians 15), multitudes of eyewitnesses (vs. 6-7) and historical documentation. Josephus, a Jewish historian for Rome wrote the following:

> Now, there was about this time Jesus, a wise man, if it be lawful to call him a man, for he was a doer of wonderful works—a teacher of such men as receive the truth with pleasure. He drew over to him both many of the Jews, and many of the Gentiles. He was [the] Christ; (64) and when Pilate, at the suggestion of the principal men amongst us, had condemned him to the cross, □ those that loved him at the first did not forsake him, for he appeared to them alive again the third day, □ as the divine prophets had foretold these and ten thousand other wonderful things concerning him; and the tribe of Christians, so named from him, are not extinct at this day.[1]

It is important to note that Jesus was physically born into this world, physically He died and physically He rose from the dead to ascend into Heaven.

---

[1] Josephus, F., & Whiston, W. (1996, c1987). *The works of Josephus : Complete and unabridged*. Includes index. (Ant 18.63-64). Peabody: Hendrickson.

Thought Questions

1. Why do books like 1 John focus so much on the humanity of Jesus Christ?

2. How can you prove the Deity of Christ?

3. Why is it important that Jesus Christ is fully God and fully man?

4. You are talking to a Jehovah Witness and they state that Christ never claimed to be God. How would you answer them?

5. How could you use this lesson to explain Jesus Christ to a Jewish person?

Lesson 5

I. Creation of Man

Man was directly and immediately created by God on the sixth day of creation, with appearance of age, in God's image and likeness. Man was created free of sin with a rational nature, intelligence, volition, self-determination and moral responsibility to God (Genesis 2:7, 15-25; James 3:9). Life of all men begins at _____. The spirit of man does not exist prior to conception.

Man is distinct from animals. Man was made in the likeness of God and animals were not. Man has attributes that animals do not, i.e. God-consciousness, self-consciousness, world-consciousness, moral decision making, will, etc.. Man has some attributes that animals may have, however, man's are superior, i.e. intellect, emotion, communication, etc.. Man was created to have dominion over the animals and the earth (Genesis 1:26-28).

Men are _____ from angels in that they are a race and angels are not. This means that men cannot become angels and angels cannot become men. Men are distinct from both angels and God and will be for all eternity (1 Corinthians 6:3; Hebrews 1:14; 2:6-8; 12:22-24). Men are similar to angels in having a personality, but limited more so in power and abilities.

God's intention in the creation of man was that man should glorify God, enjoy God's fellowship, live his life in the will of God, and by this accomplish God's purpose for man in the world (Isaiah 43:7; Colossians 1:16; Revelation 4:11).

God does not call every human a "child of God". ALL people are _____ God's children. The children of God are only those who put their faith in Jesus Christ (John 1:12-13; Romans 9:7-8).

II. Sin Nature

The problem with the doctrine of the sin nature of man is that people do not want to believe that it applies to them. People want to believe that they are born spiritually and morally _____. It is the desire to disbelieve in a sin nature that makes Christianity difficult to accept. This is the reason that all false religions and cults believe that works are necessary in some form for salvation. People want to depend on their own "good" works.

The sin nature is the reality that sin has been _____ directly from Adam to every individual since Adam (except Jesus Christ, since He was without a human father) (Romans 5:12-19). The imputation of the sin nature means that each person possesses a sinful nature that is passed on from Adam to each generation. By this nature, all men are guilty of sin. The sin nature is inherited and each person is guilty of sin at the point of conception.

Every person has a sin nature and is totally depraved, in that they lack the proper affection and love toward God and they do evil. Total depravity, more importantly, refers to the fact that the whole of man was corrupted by sin, including man's _____. It does not mean that man will be as sinful as possible, for the majority of unsaved people restrain their sinfulness. Inherited sin addresses the nature of man, where imputed sin addresses the reality of that nature imputed to each person from Adam.

Adam and Eve became sinners because they sinned, where every person afterward sins because they possess a sin nature. After the fall, Adam and Eve committed sin because they now had a sin nature.

In Adam's sin of disobedience to the revealed will and Word of God, man lost his innocence; incurred the penalty of spiritual and physical death; became subject to the wrath of God; and became inherently corrupt and utterly incapable of choosing or doing that which is acceptable to God apart from divine grace (Genesis 2:16-17; 3:1-19; John 3:36; Romans 3:23; 6:23; 1 Corinthians 2:14; Ephesians 2:1-3; 1 Timothy 2:13-14; 1 John 1:8). With no recuperative powers to enable him to recover himself, man is hopelessly lost. Man's salvation is thereby wholly of God's grace through the redemptive work of our Lord Jesus Christ.

Because all men are in Adam, a nature corrupted by Adam's sin has been transmitted to all men of all ages, Jesus Christ being the only exception. All men are thus sinners by nature, by choice, and by divine declaration (Psalm 14:1-3; Jeremiah 17:9; Romans 3:9-18, 23; 5:10-12).

The results of Adam's sin were a three-fold death:

1) _____ death, which is the separation of the body from the spirit, is the particular penalty of imputed sin.

2) _____ death, which is the separation of the spirit from God (while living on earth), is particular to inherited sin. This is the state in which man is born.

3) _____ death, which is the separation of the body and spirit from God, is the particular and final penalty for depravity. Eternal death is a penalty for all unforgiven sin: inherited, imputed, impaired, committed or omitted. This is the final state of all unbelievers.

III.   Depravity of Man

The depravity of man refers to man being completely and totally _____ by sin. This depravity includes the will of man (John 8:34). Depravity is any lack of holy affection to God or any bias toward evil. Due to imputation of sin every person is a sinner and is depraved (Romans 3:10-23; 5:12). The depravity of man is a total depravity, not partial. This does not mean that an unsaved individual has no disposition or tendency to do good (John 8:9; Romans 2:14). A depraved sinner is not without some pleasing or religious qualities (Matthew 23:23; Mark 10:21). A person as totally depraved is not prone to commit every form of sin (Matthew 23:23; Romans 2:14; 2 Timothy 3:13). No sinner is as intense in sin as he could be (Genesis 15:16; Matthew 11:24; 2 Timothy 3:13).

Depravity is properly understood that a sinner is destitute of true love for God (John 5:42), elevates some lower affection above God (2 Timothy 3:4), prefers self to God (2 Timothy 3:2), is at enmity with God (Romans 8:7), corrupted in every faculty (2 Corinthians 7:1, Ephesians 4:18; Titus 1:15; Hebrews 3:12), can do nothing God can fully approve of (Isaiah 64:6; Romans 3:9; 7:18) and has a pervading tendency toward greater depravity (Romans 7:18, 23). Total depravity is not total inability. A sinner is restricted, but still is sovereign over that which God has placed man over. A sinner is limited and unable to change their course of life, prefer God to self, neither live above sin nor capable of performing any act fully acceptable to God.

IV. Origin of Sin

The origin of sin was committed, at a minimum, by Satan (Isaiah 14:12-17; Ezekiel 28:11-19). Scripture does not state when the demons fell, whether it was with Satan or some time after. Man's sin was by an historical act that God used to test man (Genesis 3). Satan's sin was the original sin of creation, man's sin was the original sin of the human race (Romans 5:12). Satan's sin was internal were man's sin was influenced by the serpent (Genesis 3). Adam's sin was deliberate, where Eve was deceived (1 Timothy 2:14).

The fall of Satan reveals that both man and angels were created with the ability to choose from moral alternatives. A desire to sin arose in Satan. The first sin was rebellion against God's authority and pride in both man's and the angel's potential. Both man and angels are fully accountable for their own sin. They were not tempted by God nor did He create sin (James 1:13).

V. Extent of Sin

The extent of sin affects all of creation. When Eve sinned the affects were not realized until Adam's sin (Genesis 3:6-7). Upon Adam's sin, the creation began to experience the affects of sin (Genesis 3:17-19). Therefore, Adam's sin extended to the entire universe as it began to physically decay. By the time after the flood the full affects of sin on creation were experienced. The extent of sin in angels is seen in that they are confirmed in holiness or sinfulness for all eternity. The extent of sin in man is revealed in the depravity of man.

VI. Imputation of Sin

Imputation of sin is the inheriting of the sin nature directly from Adam (Romans 5:12-19). This one act caused a sin nature in every man, even before there was a written law to explain the penalties. The immediate result of that one act of sin was death, physical, spiritual and ultimately eternal. This death has been passed on to everyone from generation to generation, even to those not conscience. Finally, that by this one act of sin there was also one act of righteousness by Christ that remedies the act of Adam. The contrast in Romans 5:12-19 parallels the sin of Adam and the salvation of Christ. It reveals the similarities and differences between the two events in history. The sin of Adam was a real event and test in history, not a mythical account.

The parallels between Adam and Christ are seen in the "oneness". The result of Adam's sin was both physical and spiritual death. The "oneness" is revealed in the one sinful act of Adam and the one righteous act of Christ. The sin nature extends to all people, except Christ. Sin was brought into the world by one sinful act not acts. Thus, Christ's death was one act for one act, not one act for many acts. Therefore, Christ died by one act for sin, not sins.

Due to Adam's one sin, all men are rightly judged for imputed sin. It is deserved and to all. However, grace is not to all men and completely and totally unmerited by men. Because of this, not all men are in Christ, but all men are born in Adam. The result of being in Adam is _____ where the imputation of righteousness by being in Christ is _____. Those in Adam have a certain death both physical and spiritual. However, those in Christ do not have a spiritual death any longer and may even avoid the physical death in the rapture.

Now that we see the parallels and differences we can see that there is a similarity and even more so a superiority between Christ and Adam. There is a similarity in all being "in Adam" and those "in Christ"; the one act of Adam and one act of Christ; the union with Adam and those in union with Christ. However, the superiority is in the nature of the one act of Christ, which can impute His righteousness to those who are in Adam. Christ's one act is the remedy for the result of Adam's one act. The important note between the similarity in oneness between Adam and Christ is in a "natural oneness" verses a "spiritual oneness". All people are in Adam (naturally) and some people are in Christ (spiritually).

The superiority can be seen in the contrast between Adam and Christ. Adam disobeyed and Christ obeyed. Adam's act was imputed to all people; Christ's righteous act is imputed to few people. Adam's act has the involvement and participation of each person and Christ's act has the involvement and participation of only Christ and not any man.

There is a contrast in union as described above in that Adam's is a natural union and Christ's is a spiritual one. The union with Adam is immediate at conception and the union with Christ is conditional based upon faith and regeneration. All suffer through Adam because of his act and only Christ suffered by His act.

No one can escape the imputation of sin but few receive the imputation of righteousness. Therefore, all men deserve of the imputation of sin and its judgment but none are deserving of the grace of God. Thus, all sin is merited and grace is completely unmerited.

VII. Answering Objections

There are some objections raised that can be easily answered. First, there is the objection that there is no sin prior to "consciousness". However, most sin is of nature rather than deliberate. Also, the first act of an infant is a self-act of desiring milk and the result is crying. That cry for milk is an act of selfishness, which is all an infant knows. Thus, the very first act of an infant is selfish although the infant is not conscious of sin. Nobody ever had to teach a child to sin. At the earliest age children will test what they know is wrong. As soon as a child can speak, they start lying. These are examples of sins from a sin nature that they know prior to "consciousness".

The second objection is that we cannot be responsible for what Adam did. However, we are responsible for what we do, and because of Adam we have a sin nature, and therefore we sin. It is our sin that we are responsible for, to God.

This can be followed with the objection that we cannot repent of Adam's sin. However, it is because of sin and not sins (plural) that we need to repent. Can we be guilty of all Adam's sins? Adam made one choice that gave him and every person to follow him a sin nature. We are not guilty of Adam's sins but our own sin.

Although Adam's one sinful act brought about a sin nature in that all sin, one righteous act of Christ brought about the availability for any to have His righteousness imputed to them. Where the sin nature is once to all, righteousness is once to few.

Thought Questions

1. Why is it so important to explain man's sinfulness when explaining the gospel?

2. Why is the doctrine of the sin nature of man difficult for many people to believe?

3. How are men and animals different?

4. A friend states that they just watched a television program were a person became an angel to help others. They ask your thoughts on people becoming angels. How do you answer?

5. Does man have the ability to choose God apart from God? Is their will truly "free"?

Lesson 6

Creation, Fall, and Promise

I. **Genesis: The First Three Chapters**

The first three chapters of Genesis cover:

     1. God's _____ _____ (Genesis 1 and Genesis 2),

     2. The _____ (Genesis 3),

     3. The _____ over all creation (Genesis 3), and

     4. God's _____ _____ _____ (Genesis 3:15)

At the end of day 6, His Creation was deemed perfect:

(Read) "And God saw everything that he had made, and, behold, it was _____ _____. And there was evening and there was morning, the sixth day." (Genesis 1:31)

Genesis 2 tells us of the one main command given to Adam.

(Question: Was Eve formed yet at the time of this command?)

(Read) "And the Lord God commanded the man, saying, 'You may surely eat of every tree of the garden, but of the tree of the knowledge of good and evil you shall not eat, for in the day that you eat of it you shall surely die.'" (Genesis 2:16-17)

(Major point to understand: This death was both _____ and _____. Proof of this is in Genesis 3.)

(Read Genesis 3:1) "Now the serpent was more crafty than any other beast of the field that the Lord God had made. He said to the woman, 'Did God actually say, 'You shall not eat of any tree in the garden'?'"

(Question: Did the serpent, which knew God's command to Adam, say it correctly to Eve?)

(Read Genesis 3:2-3) "And the woman said unto the serpent, 'We may eat of the fruit of the trees in the garden, but God said, 'You shall not eat of the fruit of the tree that is in the midst of the garden, neither shall you touch it, lest you die'.'"

(Question: Did Eve get God's original command to Adam correct?)

(Read Genesis 3:4-5) "But the serpent said to the woman, 'You will not surely die. For God knows that when you eat of it your eyes will be opened, and you will be like God, knowing good and evil'."

(Discuss: How is what transpired in Genesis 3:1-5 similar to that of professing Christians and the myriad of false teachers today, like Joel Osteen, TD Jakes, Ken Copeland, and Bill Johnson? 2 main points should be obvious)

(Read Genesis 3:6-7) "So when the woman saw that the tree was good for food, and that it was a delight to the eyes, and that the tree was to be desired to make one wise, she took of its fruit and ate, and she also gave some to her husband who was with her, and he ate. Then the eyes of both were opened, and they knew that they were naked. And they sewed fig leaves together and made themselves loincloths." (Genesis 3:6-7)

Their eyes were opened, thus they immediately _____ _____.

(Discuss how the reaction of Adam and Eve to "cover themselves" and "hide" is just like what we do today when we sin.)

II.   Genesis: The Fall and the Promise

Because of this original sin, we now see all the bad entering the world, including death, disease, suffering, extinction, thorns and thistles, and so on. _____ of _____ was affected! (Romans 8)

Rather than taking responsibility for their actions, Adam _____ Eve, and Eve _____ the serpent. (Genesis 3:12-13)

3 results of the curse on creation were mentioned in Genesis 3:14-19. (Discuss)

     1.

     2.

     3.

Immediate spiritual death occurred when the forbidden fruit was eaten. However, Scripture is clear that _____ _____ would be the end result of original sin.

(Read Genesis 3:19) "By the sweat of your face you shall eat bread, till you return to the ground, for out of it you were taken; for you are dust, and to dust you shall return."

(Read Genesis 3:15) "And I will put enmity between thee and the woman, and between thy seed and her seed; it shall bruise thy head, and thou shalt bruise his heel."

Who is the seed of the serpent? _____

Who is the seed of Eve (making Biblical genealogies so vital to understand)?_____ _____

In between the verses regarding immediate spiritual death and the promise of future physical death, God gives us the first prophecy of the coming _____! (Genesis 3:15)

(Read Genesis 3:21) "And the Lord God made for Adam and for his wife garments   of skins and clothed them."

(Discussion questions)

1. What did the nakedness of Adam and Eve represent?

2. What was the initial response to their nakedness?

3. What did God use to cover the nakedness of Adam and Eve?

4. What did this mark the start of in the OT?

5. This was a foreshadowing of?

A literal interpretation of the beginning of Genesis is vital to a correct understanding of the rest of the Bible.

   1. God's plan of _____ is based on what happened in Genesis.

   2. The Bible teaches that _____ _____ is only a result of sin.

   3.Because physical death is the result of sin, death _____ _____ have been present before Adam and Eve's original sin.

   4.Therefore, we can conclude that _____-_____-_____ _____ never happened, as it requires death to always have been present! In fact, death would have to have been present for billions of years before Original Sin about 6000 years ago.

(Discuss the next question as time allows, as this answer appears later in the book) With the knowledge that you have gained so far,

"Why did Jesus have to die?"

Lesson 7

Salvation

Salvation is wholly of God _____ by grace _____ through faith _____ by the redemption of Jesus Christ _____, the merit of His shed blood, and not based on human merit or works (John 1:12; Ephesians 1:7; 2:8-10; 1 Peter 1:18-19). It is this one doctrine that makes Christianity different from ALL others. Christianity believes that there is NO work from man that can save a person nor assist God in the salvation. The doctrine of salvation is the one doctrine that is both eternally important to get accurate and unique to Christianity. All religion can be classified into two categories; the merit of man (works salvation) or the grace of God (imputed righteousness). All religions except Christianity fit in the merit of man.

Salvation is often confusing because many people use the word "salvation" to mean many different things. There are several aspects covered by the word "salvation". It could refer to the entire salvation process from the convicting work of the Holy Spirit to the glorification of man in Heaven. Sometimes, people use the phrase to refer specifically to the act of regeneration or to speak of someone coming to faith. It is the broad use of the word "salvation" that causes much of the confusion.

Salvation is a process that starts with the Holy Spirit convicting the heart of a sinner to draw them to repentance and ends with a believer's glorification upon entrance into Heaven. Many have a problem because they do not understand that the Holy Spirit convicts sinners prior to the specific act of salvation. A sinner can reject or resist the convicting work of the Holy Spirit. This is not the same as resisting the grace of salvation.

The specific act of salvation involves many simultaneous aspects of doctrine. The many aspects of salvation include regeneration, conversion, repentance, faith, justification, Spirit baptism and indwelling of the Holy Spirit. These occur simultaneous and immediately at the point of salvation. There are ongoing aspects of salvation that start at the point of salvation and continue until glorification, they include: sanctification and perseverance. The final act of salvation is glorification in heaven, when believers receive a sinless existence (body and spirit).

It is important to understand that there is no chronological order to the aspects of salvation. A person does not believe and then get regenerated nor does God regenerate a person so then they can believe. These acts are simultaneous. Humans may not have the ability to understand how these acts can be simultaneous, however, that is how Scripture teaches this doctrine (Romans 9-10).

When considering the many different aspects of salvation it is good to think in terms of the following four areas:

1) Where does the activity take place, on earth or in Heaven?

2) Is the activity for all believers or only for church age believers?

3) Who is the agent of activity, God or man?

4) What is the type of activity, one of experiential or judicial?

These areas may help us to see the multiple dimensions of the terms use for salvation. The chart below should be of assistance in showing the different facets of salvation.

	AREA OF ACTIVITY	DISPENSATION OF ACTIVITY	AGENT OF ACTIVITY	TYPE OF ACTIVITY
Election	Heaven	All	Divine	Judicial
Regeneration	Earth	All	Divine	Experiential
Conversion (Repentance and Faith)	Earth	All	Human	Experiential
Justification	Heaven	All	Divine	Judicial
Adoption	Earth & Heaven	All	Divine	Judicial
Spirit Baptism	Earth & Heaven	Church	Divine	Judicial
Indwelling	Earth	Church	Divine	Experiential
Sanctification	Earth	All	Divine	Experiential
Perseverance	Earth	All	Human	Experiential
Glorification	Heaven	All	Divine	Experiential

I. Election

Election is the act of God by which, before the foundation of the world, He chose in Christ those whom He graciously regenerates, saves, and sanctifies (Romans 8:28-30; Ephesians 1:4-11; 2 Thessalonians 2:13; 2 Timothy 2:10; 1 Peter 1:1-2). Some may argue that election is the first step in the process of salvation. To an extent that is correct and not correct. When discussing the election it must be understood that it is a doctrine of God, who is not bound by time. Therefore, God uses phrases like *"elect before the foundation of the earth"* (Ephesians 1:4) to explain to man something that man cannot understand. Election occurs outside of time. Therefore, it cannot truly be placed in a chronological order.

Sovereign election does not contradict or negate the responsibility of man to repent and trust Christ as Savior and Lord (Ezekiel 18:23, 32; 33:11; John 3:18-19, 36; 5:40; Romans 9:22-23; 2 Thessalonians 2:10-12; Revelation 22:17). Nevertheless, since sovereign grace includes the means of receiving the gift of salvation as well as the gift itself, sovereign election will result in what God determines. All whom the Father calls to Himself will come in faith and all who come in faith the Father will receive (John 6:37-40, 44; Acts 13:48; James 4:8).

The unmerited favor that God grants to totally depraved sinners is not related to any initiative of their own part nor to God's anticipation of what they might do by their own will, but is solely of His sovereign grace and mercy (Ephesians 1:4-7; Titus 3:4-7; 1 Peter 1:2).

Election should not be looked upon as based merely on abstract sovereignty. God is truly sovereign but He exercises this sovereignty in harmony with His other attributes, especially His omniscience, justice, holiness, wisdom, grace and love (Romans 9:11-16). This sovereignty will always exalt the will of God in a manner totally consistent with His character as revealed in the life of our Lord Jesus Christ (Matthew 11:25-28; 2 Timothy 1:9).

Regeneration

Regeneration is a _____ work of the Holy Spirit by which a new nature and eternal life are given (John 3:3-7; Titus 3:5). It is the new life implanted in the heart of a believer and is the restoration of the original God given tendencies toward God before the fall. After the fall, man's will is to sin. After regeneration, man's will is to glorify God.

Regeneration is instantaneous and is accomplished solely by the power of the Holy Spirit through the instrumentality of the Word of God (John 5:24), when the repentant sinner, as enabled by the Holy Spirit, responds in faith to the divine provision of salvation. Regeneration is not based on any works of man nor is it assisted by man's works.

Genuine regeneration is manifested by fruits worthy of repentance as demonstrated in righteous attitudes and conduct. Good works will be its proper evidence and fruit (1 Corinthians 6:19-20; Ephesians 2:10), and will be experienced to the extent that the believer submits to the control of the Holy Spirit in his life through faithful obedience to the Word of God (Ephesians 5:17-21; Philippians 2:12b; Colossians 3:16; 2 Peter 1:4-10). This obedience causes the believer to be increasingly conformed to the image of our Lord Jesus Christ (2 Corinthians 3:18). Such a conformity is climaxed in the believer's glorification at Christ's coming (Romans 8:17; 2 Peter 1:4; 1 John 3:2 3).

III. Conversion

Conversion is man's _____ turning from sin to God. Conversion is a two fold turning, first from sin and second to God. Conversion is man's confession and belief (Romans 10:9-10). There are two characteristics that describe conversion; repentance and faith.

A.   Repentance

Repentance is intellectually, emotionally and voluntary turning from _____. At the fall man became corrupt intellectually, emotionally and voluntary. The turning to God must also involve all three, because that is the entire makeup of man. This is usually the cause of contention with some, in that, they believe that man cannot repent until these three parts of man are regenerated. However, due to the reality that regeneration and repentance occur simultaneously, the intellect, emotion and will are regenerated at the same point of repentance.

Many people can intellectually understand a need to turn from sin. Some even have the capacity to be emotional about it. Only those whose volition (will) is changed (regeneration) experience salvation. Repentance is God's desire for all men (Acts 17:30; 2 Peter 3:9).

B.   *Faith*

Faith is intellectually, emotionally and voluntary turning to
_____. Some would believe that faith is capable within the nature of man. That man has the capacity to turn to God. This stems from a false view of the affects of the fall on man. Man cannot within himself turn to God intellectually, emotionally and voluntary.

Many people can intellectually understand a need to turn to God and the gospel. Some even have the capacity to be emotional about it. Only those whose volition (will) is changed (regeneration) experience salvation. Many people, such as Pelagius, struggle with the concept of total depravity because man is able to understand at least intellectually and/or emotionally the Gospel of God and therefore assumes that man can volitionally turn to God.

Justification

Justification before God is an act of God (Romans 8:33) by which He legally declares righteous those who, through faith in Christ alone, repent of their sins (Luke 13:3; Acts 2:38; 3:19; 11:18; Romans 2:4; 2 Corinthians 7:10; Isaiah 55:6-7) and confess Him as sovereign Lord (Romans 10:9-10; 1 Corinthians 12:3; 2 Corinthians 4:5; Philippians 2:11). Justification is being declared just; no longer condemned. It is the declaring of one as righteous. It does not change one's spiritual condition making one righteous (i.e. perfectly holy in the present age). This righteousness is apart from any virtue or work of man (Romans 3:20; 4:6) and involves the imputation of our _____ to Christ (Colossians 2:14; 1 Peter 2:24) and the imputation of Christ's _____ to us (1 Corinthians 1:30; 2 Corinthians 5:21). By this we mean God is enabled to *"be just and the justifier of the one who has faith in Jesus"* (Romans 3:26). Only God, as judge, can declare one as just.

V.   Sanctification

Sanctification is the growth of the implanted new nature (it follows regeneration). It is natural to all things to _____ after they are born. The same is true in the spiritual realm. This is a continuing consequence of union with Christ. Therefore, there is a logical and chronological order to sanctification, which occurs only after regeneration. Something must be born before it can grow.

Sanctification is a continuing process of the believer developing to be more like Christ. This process is never complete until the death of the body.

Every believer is sanctified (set apart) unto God by justification and is therefore declared to be holy and identified as a saint. Sanctification is positional and instantaneous and should not be confused with progressive sanctification. Sanctification has to do with the believer's standing, not his present walk or condition (Acts 20:32; 1 Corinthians 1:2, 30; 6:11; 2 Thessalonians 2:13; Hebrews 2:11; 3:1; 10:10, 14; 13:12; 1 Peter 1:2).

There is also, by the work of the Holy Spirit, a progressive sanctification by which the state of the believer is brought closer to the standing that the believer positionally enjoys through justification. Through obedience to the Word of God and the empowering of the Holy Spirit, the believer is able to live a life of increasing holiness in conformity to the will of God, becoming more and more like our Lord Jesus Christ (John 17:17, 19; Romans 6:1-22; 2 Corinthians 3:18; 1 Thessalonians 4:3-4; 5:23).

In this respect, every saved person is involved in a daily conflict, the new creation in Christ doing battle against the flesh, but adequate provision is made for victory through the power of the indwelling Holy Spirit. This struggle nevertheless stays with the believer all through this earthly life and is never completely ended. All claims to the eradication of sin in this life are unscriptural. Eradication of sin is not possible, but the Holy Spirit does provide for victory over sin (Galatians 5:16-25; Ephesians 4:22-24; Philippians 3:12; Colossians 3:9-10; 1 Peter 1:14-16; 1 John 3:5-9).

VI.   Perseverance

Perseverance is the _____ continuing in the faith. Perseverance is the human side of sanctification. Likewise, perseverance can only occur after regeneration. Whereas sanctification measures the degrees of maturity, perseverance measures the degrees of yielding and assurance measures the degrees of confidence.

All the redeemed, once saved, are kept by God's power and are thus eternally secure in Christ forever and will persevere (John 5:24; 6:37-40; 10:27-30; Romans 5:9-10; 8:1, 31-39; 1 Corinthians 1:4-8; Ephesians 4:30; Hebrews 7:25; 13:5; 1 Peter 1:5; Jude 24). It is the privilege of believers to rejoice in the assurance of their salvation through the testimony of God's Word, which, however, clearly forbids the use of Christian liberty as an occasion for sinful living and carnality (Romans 6:15-22; 13:13-14; Galatians 5:13, 25-26; Titus 2:11-14).

Thought Questions

1. What is it that makes Christianity's view of salvation different from all other religions?

2. A coworker states that it does not matter what you believe as long as you live a good life, God will take you with Him to Heaven. How would you respond to this person?

3. During a Bible study two Christians start to debate concerning which act of salvation comes first chronologically, regeneration or belief. How could you help them to understand the importance Scripture makes on this subject?

4. An old friend calls you up and states they became a Christian, but their lifestyle has not changed. They state that they do not need to change as long as they believe in God. Is this statement true? How would you answer this friend?

5. A member of your church states that they are not sure they are saved because they struggle with sin in their life. How can you help them?

Lesson 8

The Church

I. Definition

The term most often translated "church" is ἐκκλησία (ekklēsía) in the Greek. This term has the meaning of an assembly or congregation and appears over 100 times in the New Testament. The Greek translation of the Hebrew Old Testament, called the Septuagint, most often translates ἐκκλησία as קָהָל

(qā·hāl). קָהָל is used over 57 times of the 97 uses of ἐκκλησία in the Old Testament (Septuagint) and refers to an assembly, congregation, army, or crowd.

ἐκκλησία had several meanings in the first century:

A. *a regularly summoned legislative body or assembly*

B. *a casual gathering of people or an assemblage*

C. *people with shared belief, community, or congregation*

In regards to the biblical history of the word ἐκκλησία, it originally meant any public assembly of citizens summoned by a herald.

II. Early Church

When Paul spoke of the church, he did so without thought of _____ congregations, but as one church. Though Paul wrote to individual groups of congregations that were recognized as separate and distinct, he also saw the true believers as one church. As the congregations of believers met for the purpose of the worship of God, the term church started to have a more specific meaning, denoting a specific group of people who function in a specific manner.

Thus, the word ἐκκλησία took on a new and more specifically Christian meaning. It no longer referred to a general gathering or assembly of people, but to a group that meets for the _____ of God, the reading and explaining of His Word, and the practicing of the ordinances (baptism and communion). It also referred to the purity of the group, i.e., church discipline, but we must note that the early church did not seem to make much of a distinction between different local congregations.

III.   Church of the Middle Ages

As the church moved into the Middle Ages, theologians started to be more specific about the meaning of the church by making a distinction between what they called the "visible church" and the "invisible church," or the _____ and _____ church respectively. This distinction was made to refer to the body of all believers in Jesus Christ (invisible church), and those local congregations who met for the worship of God but could have unbelievers in their midst (visible church).

A.   *Invisible or Universal Church*

The invisible or universal church is the body of believers everywhere in the world throughout time. The universal church is made up of only and _____ believers.

B.   *Visible or Local Church*

The second distinction is the local or visible church. This reference to the church is the local gathering of people for the purpose of fulfilling the function of the church. However, unlike the universal church, this reference to the church can refer to a group of people, but this group of people is not exclusively made up of converted believers in Jesus Christ. The local church refers to a local congregation of people, _____ and _____, who gather regularly for the purpose of the worship of God.

IV.   The Reformation Church

During the Reformation, the Puritans definition of the church was based on three functions of the church:

1) The proclamation of the _____ _____ _____,

2) The practice of the _____ (i.e., baptism and communion), and

3) The purity of the church through church _____.

V.   Modern Church

In the recent age, with the rise of Dispensationalism, the definition of the church had, once again, been further clarified and specified. An evaluation of the long-held Roman Catholic teaching of Israel as the Old Testament church was being rethought. Dispensationalism made a differentiation between Old Testament Israel and the New Testament church. They saw a discontinuity between Israel and the church.

According to this thought, _____ is not the _____ and the church is not Israel. This does not change the previous definitions of the church and would agree with the covenant definition of the church; but it limits the definition to the New Testament church and does not trace this definition back into Old Testament Israel. This distinction helps to further clarify the definition of the church developed so far throughout history, but it applies this definition only to those believers after Pentecost, locally gathering for the function of the church.

Throughout history, we see the progression of the definition of "the church" move from a general term referring to any gathering of people to a very specific definition referring to a special group of people, the function of those people, and, finally, also the time period in which they lived.

Thought Questions

1. What was the view of the church in the first century?

2. How did view of the church change during the middle ages?

3. How did the definition change for the church during the reformation?

4. How has the definition of the church changed over time?

5. Is the church a building or the people

Lesson 9

Eternal State

The eternal state is the conscious state in which man will live, both body and soul for all eternity. The aspects that Christians needs to address are death, the intermediate state and the final eternal state. There is much confusion on these subjects.

I. Death

The concept of death is _____. Death is the result of sin. There are three types of death: physical, spiritual and eternal. Physical death is the separation of the _____ from the _____. The soul does NOT cease to exist, but is released from the body. The remedy for physical death is the resurrection, when the body will rejoin the soul.

The second type of death is spiritual death. Spiritual death is the separation of man from a _____ with God (Ephesians 2:1-3). It is spiritual death that was the consequence of Adam's sin of eating the fruit of the tree of the knowledge of good and evil (Genesis 2:17). All humans are born in this state. The remedy for spiritual death is salvation.

The last type of death is eternal death, also called the *"second death"* (Revelation 2:11; 20:6, 14; 21:8). Eternal death is the _____ separation of man from a relationship with God (Revelation 20:14-15; 21:8). This is the permanent result of spiritual death and the rejection of God's saving grace. There is _____ remedy for eternal death. There are no second chances for spiritual life after physical death.

II. Intermediate State

The intermediate state is the _____ existence of the personality of both the godly and ungodly between the time of physical death and the resurrection at the Great White Throne Judgment. Physical death involves no loss of our immaterial consciousness (Revelation 6:9-11), the soul of the redeemed passes immediately into the presence of Christ (Luke 23:43; Philippians 1:23; 2 Corinthians 5:8), there is a separation of soul and body (Philippians 1:21-24), and for the redeemed, such separation will continue until the rapture (1 Thessalonians 4:13-17), which initiates the first resurrection (Revelation 20:4-6), when our soul and body will be reunited to be glorified forever with our Lord (Philippians 3:21; 1 Corinthians 15:35-44, 50-54). Until that time, the souls of the redeemed in Christ remain in joyful fellowship with our Lord Jesus Christ (2 Corinthians 5:8).

A.   *Heaven*

The righteous at death _____ enter into the presence of God (Ecclesiastes 12:7; Luke 23:43; 2 Corinthians 5:1-8). Christ told the thief on the cross next to Him, that he would be in paradise that very day when he died (Luke 23:43). Heaven is a temporary place of rest for the saints until the final rest in the eternal state (Revelation 14:13).

B.   *Hell*

The wicked, unbelievers, at physical death _____ enter into hell, which is a place of restriction (1 Peter 3:19). Hell is a literal place where the soul consciously endures continuous torment as a consequence of sin (Luke 16:19-31; Mark 9:44, 46, 48; 2 Peter 2:9). Hell is different then the Lake of Fire. There are different degrees of punishment in hell based upon the amount of knowledge of the Word of God one had on earth (Matthew 11:24; Luke 12:47-48; Romans 2:12).

III.   Eternal state

The eternal state is ushered in by the Great White Throne Judgment (Revelation 20:11-15). There will be a bodily resurrection of all men, the saved to eternal life (John 6:39; Romans 8:10-11, 19-23; 2 Corinthians 4:14), and the unsaved to judgment and everlasting punishment (Daniel 12:2; John 5:29; Revelation 20:13-15).

The souls of the unsaved at death are kept under punishment until the second resurrection (Luke 16:19-26; Revelation 20:13-15), when the soul and the resurrection body will be united (John 5:28-29). They shall then appear at the Great White Throne Judgment (Revelation 20:11-15) and shall be cast into the lake of fire (Matthew 25:41-46), cut off from the life of God forever (Daniel 12:2; Matthew 25:41-46; 2 Thessalonians 1:7-9).

A.   *New Heaven, New Earth and New Jerusalem*

There is a literal place known as heaven, were persons, both men and angels, will consciously _____ God in the real, everlasting presence of God. This will be a place where God is the center of all worship and purpose for being and not for the enjoyment of man. People will enjoy worshiping God but it is not a place about man, but God.

There will be no marriage (Matthew 22:30; Mark 12:25). Therefore, there is a change in our human relationships on earth. We will not continue in the same relationship structure that we had on earth. Although we will see family members the relationship will be changed, because the focus will be on God and not man.

Judgment is based on having your name in the *"Lamb's book of life"* (Revelation 3:5; 13:8; 17:8; 20:15; 21:27; 22:19).

B.   *The Lake of Fire*

There is a literal place known as hell or the lake of fire, were persons, both men and angels, will be consciously _____, both body (for men) and soul, for their sin in a real, everlasting, tormenting lake of fire.

Hell is a temporary place of punishment until the Great White Throne Judgment (Revelation 20:11-15). The inhabitants of Hell are cast into the Lake of Fire for all eternity (Revelation 20:14; 21:8).

Judgment is based on works (Revelation 20:12). The problem with works is that there are no good works that can merit salvation (Isaiah 64:4; Ephesians 2:8-9; Titus 3:5).

Thought Questions

1. Do you believe in a literal place called hell? Why or why not?

2. Will everyone on earth go to Heaven?

3. A friend states that they cannot believe that a loving God could send people to hell? How could you respond?

4. A member of the Church of Latter Day Saints tells you that they will enter into eternity with their spouses and children. How could you correct them?

5. A Jehovah Witness tells you that they cannot accept an everlasting punishment. What could you share with this person?

WHAT DO WE BELIEVE?

A SYSTEMATIC THEOLOGY OF THE CHRISTIAN FAITH

ANDREW R. RAPPAPORT

FOREWORD BY PHIL JOHNSON

www.StrivingForEternity.org

www.ingramcontent.com/pod-product-compliance
Lightning Source LLC
Chambersburg PA
CBHW081651270326
41933CB00018B/3429

* 9 7 8 1 9 5 3 8 8 6 0 4 0 *